World War I

Author: Janie Doss
Editor: Mary Dieterich
Proofreaders: Cindy Neisen and Margaret Brown

COPYRIGHT © 2017 Mark Twain Media, Inc.

ISBN 978-1-62223-646-6

Printing No. CD-404267

Mark Twain Media, Inc., Publishers
Distributed by Carson-Dellosa Publishing LLC

Table of Contents

Note to the Teacher ii
Teacher Pages 1
World War I Alliances 4
Colonies of Africa 1914 7
The Von Schlieffen Plan 8
Trench Life 9
Differing Points of View 12
"Break of Day in the Trenches" by Isaac
    Rosenberg 14
Unrestricted Submarine Warfare 16
Weapons of World War I 18
Battles of World War I 21
Christmas Truce 22

The United States of America's Neutrality 23
The *Lusitania* 25
The Zimmerman Telegram 26
Really Neutral? 28
Anti-War Movement 31
Wilson's Fourteen-Point Plan 32
The Treaty of Versailles 34
Was the Treaty of Versailles Fair? 36
The Price Paid for War 38
Propaganda of World War I 39
Remembering the War 41
Answer Keys 42

Note to the Teacher

The year 2017 marks the 100th anniversary of the United States entering into World War I, and 2018 is the 100th anniversary of the ending of this world war. These two events provide a once-in-a-lifetime opportunity for students to learn about the First World War during these historic anniversary years.

World War I is a comprehensive World War I resource and activity book designed for both middle school and high school. It contains activities on the causes of World War I, daily life of the soldier, weapons, battles, the Treaty of Versailles, the United States' involvement, and war propaganda. *World War I* consists of 21 different activities that can be done individually by the students, in small groups, or in whole-class teaching. The activities each have web-based research components and a writing activity. The writing activity is designed to check student comprehension and provide an opportunity for higher-level thinking. These activities are meant to supplement or enhance the classroom curriculum. The activities can be taught within the English Language Arts or Social Studies content areas or as interdisciplinary activities, allowing for cross-curricular teacher cooperation. The activities address both Social Studies and Communication Arts standards.

The book contains
- Teacher pages that provide teaching directions with an introduction, assignment, and closure for each activity.
- Student pages that provide opportunities to conduct research, examine primary sources, interpret graphs and maps, and respond to short-answer or constructed-response questions.
- An answer key that provides suggestions for possible answers. Many of the questions are open ended, and the teacher will need to use her/his own judgment in grading the responses.

Teacher Pages

Note: Be sure to check all URLs to make sure the websites are still active. You may have to search for the latest sites or alternative sites as changes are made over time.

Hook: Display several photographs of World War I cemeteries. Choose photographs containing a large number of tomb (grave) markers. Exclude any with text that could bias the discussion. A variety of photographs can be found at the following website **URL:** <http://www.ww1wargraves.co.uk/ww1_cemeteries/Index.asp>

World War I Alliances (pg. 4–6)
- Introduction: Brainstorm possible causes for the number of markers found in the photographs (diseases, war, famine, etc.) Explain they are markers used to identify the graves of World War I soldiers. Discuss the possible causes of a war so large it is referred to as the Great War.
- Assignment: Students research pre-1914 European alliances and use the information to complete the "World War I Alliances" pages.
- Closure: Discuss the different alliances that were formed before the beginning of World War I. Discuss how these alliances were instrumental in deciding the two sides: Allied and Central Powers. Discuss the political cartoon and how it expresses Germany's opinion on the fairness of the sides.

Colonies of Africa 1914 (pg. 7)
- Introduction: Discuss the definitions of *imperialism* and *colony* at the top of "Colonies of Africa 1914" activity page.
- Assignment: Discuss generalization about the information from the chart. Consider things such as number of colonies, increase of landmass, and location of colonies. Students go online and use information from the map titled *Africa, colonial partition, to 1914* to complete the "Colonies of Africa 1914" activity.
- Closure: Students debate their choices for the most powerful country.

The Von Schlieffen Plan (pg. 8)
- Introduction: Display a photograph of Alfred Von Schlieffen. Portrait available at the website URL listed below. Brainstorm possible reasons why this man is important in causing World War I.
  URL: <http://germanhistorydocs.ghi-dc.org/sub_image.cfm?image_id=1706>
- Assignment: Students watch youtube video, *The Schlieffen Plan–And Why It Failed I THE GREAT WAR Special feat* and take notes to complete "Why Did the Von Schlieffen Plan Fail?" activity.
- Closure: Discuss the reasons students think the Von Schlieffen Plan failed and how the plan helped cause World War I.

Trench Life (pg. 9–11)
- Introduction: Discuss their perception of what life was like in the trenches.
- Assignment: Using the website URL complete the questions.
- Closure: Class discusses trench life during World War I.

Differing Points of View (pg. 12–13)
- Introduction: Read the poems out loud.
- Assignment: If students are unfamiliar with analyzing a poem, complete the activity worksheet as a class; otherwise, small groups or individually.
- Closure: As a class, discuss the answers to the activity worksheet and their opinions of the poems.

"Break of Day in the Trenches" by Isaac Rosenberg (pg. 14–15)
- Introduction: Replay the last part of the video used in "Trench Life"
  URL: <https://www.youtube.com/watch?v=P92guhd7d-8>
- Assignment: If students are unfamiliar with analyzing a poem, complete the activity worksheet as a class; otherwise, small groups or individually.
- Closure: As a class, discuss initial thoughts and poem summary. Share illustrations.

Teacher Pages (cont.)

Unrestricted Submarine Warfare (pg. 16–17)
- Introduction: Discuss that not all weapons were land based. Read over Germany's declaration of unrestricted submarine warfare. Discuss what is meant by "unrestricted" warfare and the implications toward the Allies.
- Assignment: Students research to complete the activity.
- Closure: Have students discuss their conclusions shown by the graphs and opinions about unrestricted submarine warfare.

Weapons of World War I (pg. 18–20)
- Introduction: Discuss possible weapons used during World War I. Make a class list of the weapons suggested by the students using the website **URL:** <http://www.bbc.co.uk/guides/zs666sg> to pique interest and provide possible suggestions for the class list.
- Assignment: Students research and complete the "Weapons of World War I" chart. Next, students design a print advertisement in the style of 1914–1918 print advertising. Discuss the impacts of all the weapons researched. Students complete the essay question on the two weapons they feel most impacted the war.
- Closure: Have students share the advertisements they created for the post-1900 weapons and discuss their choices and reasons for choosing their two weapons with the most impact in the war.

Battles of World War I (pg. 21)
- Introduction: Using the website URL listed below, make a list of World War I battles.
    URL: <http://www.firstworldwar.com/battles/all.htm>
- Assignment: Have students choose a battle that they will research. Only one student per battle. Students complete "Battles of World War I" card for the battle of their choice. When finished, teacher makes copies of students' cards and distributes a set to each student. Using the map *Europe 1914,* discuss and mark the map with battle locations. Discuss if geography played a role in the outcome of the battle.
    URL: <http://www.nationalarchives.gov.uk/pathways/firstworldwar/maps/europe1914.htm>
    (May need to enlarge for all to see.)
- Closure: Brainstorm any conclusions they can draw after studying the completed map. Students may use cards as study aids. After studying, students may quiz each other over the information about the battles or teacher may design an assessment based on the battles chosen and the information teacher deems important.

Christmas Truce (pg. 22)
- Introduction: Discuss family traditions for special holidays and occasions. Bring the discussion around to Christmas and their family traditions. Discuss what it would be like to be away from family on one of the special occasions. What would they do?
- Assignment: Students research details about radio shows. After research is completed, discuss with class what a good radio drama needs. After the discussion, students research the details of the Christmas truce and discuss the details of the truce. Individually or in small groups, students begin writing a radio drama about the Christmas truce. The dramas may be from any perspective.
- Closing: Students perform the radio dramas for the class.

The United States of America's Neutrality (pg. 23–24)
- Introduction: Brainstorm America's reaction to the early stages of World War I. Is America involved? On what side? Why?
- Assignment: Students read Wilson's speech and complete questions 1–3. Next students read "Ethnic Minorities at War (USA)" and as a class discuss the article. Students answer question 4. Students complete number 5.
- Closure: Students share their letters.

The *Lusitania* (pg. 25)
- Introduction: Review what Germany's policy of submarine warfare was.
- Assignment: Use the URLs listed on the activity page to research the *Lusitania*. When research is done, continue with the activity. As a class, discuss possible differences between America's perception of the sinking and Germany's perception. Students write newspaper articles.
- Closure: Share newspaper articles.

Teacher Pages (cont.)

The Zimmerman Telegram (pg. 26–27)
- Introduction: Discuss possible reasons America might want to join in the war: economics, *Lusitania*, fear of what might happen if they don't become involved…
- Assignment: Complete the questions on the activity sheet.
- Closure: Discuss answers to the questions. Discuss if after the Zimmerman Telegram, the United States had enough reason to enter the war. Why or why not?

Really Neutral? (pg. 28–30)
- Introduction: Discuss if during wartime a country can really be neutral. Take an informal poll: Was America really neutral before April 1917? Post results.
- Assignment: Individually or in manageable groups, complete research and fill in the activity's chart. As a class discuss their findings. Discuss the essay question. Students complete essay question.
- Closure: Students share opinions and reasonings with the class. After opinions and reasons are shared, retake the poll. Discuss the results.

Anti-War Movement (pg. 31)
- Introduction: Discuss reasons for not wanting to join in the war. What groups were part of the anti-war movement?
- Assignment: Individually complete research into the anti-war movement. Individually or in small groups, students create anit-war public service messages for radio, newspaper, or television. Individuals or small groups also create anti-war propaganda posters.
- Closure: Share the messages and posters and discuss the results.

Wilson's Fourteen-Point Plan (pg. 32–33)
- Introduction: As a class, discuss what happens after a war is over.
- Assignment: Research the Fourteen-Point Plan and complete the outline. As a class, discuss the plan. Complete brochure.
- Closure: Share brochures.

The Treaty of Versailles (pg. 34–35)
- Introduction: Discuss as a class possibilities why America thought it should be the one to create the peace terms.
- Assignment: Individually or in small groups, complete research notes. As a class, discuss the similarities and differences between the treaty and Wilson's plan. Complete the chart.
- Closure: As a class, discuss which one they think is the better peace agreement.

Was the Treaty of Versailles Fair? (pg. 36–37)
- Introduction: As a class, discuss how they think the Allied powers reacted to the treaty and its terms.
- Assignment: Individually or in small groups, use the URLs listed on the activity page to complete the chart and the essay question.
- Closure: As a class, discuss opinions.

The Price Paid for War (pg. 38)
- Introduction: As a class, discuss the price paid for war: financial, emotional, physical, and loss.
- Assignment: Using the information found at the URL listed on the activity page, complete the pie charts and draw conclusions.
- Closure: Discuss the conclusions and discuss the other statistics found on the website.

Propaganda of World War I (pg. 39–40)
- Introduction: As a class, brainstorm and discuss how others try to get you to form an opinion or change your current opinion. As a class, go over the types of propaganda identified on the first page of the activity. Teacher may show the examples to the whole class, or students may look them up individually.
- Assignment: In small groups or individually, students choose examples of propaganda to analyze. (Teacher determines the number.) Students complete the analyzing worksheet.
- Closure: Class shares posters and analysis.

Remembering the War (pg. 41)
- Introduction: Discuss examples of the way World War I has been remembered (memorials, statues, gravesites…).
- Assignment: Students create a way to remember World War I.
- Closure: Share the projects.

Name: _____ Date: _____

World War I Alliances

Alliances are pacts (agreements) made between countries to "have each other's back" in disagreements and conflicts with other nations. Alliances may be public or kept secret. Alliances from as early as 1872 had a strong impact on pre-war Europe.

Directions: Using the Website URL listed below, research the six alliances listed below. Focus on the information about nations involved, the date, and the alliances made or broken.

URL: <http://www.u.arizona.edu/~salvador/Spring%20thru%20February/World%20War%201/ Causes%20of%20WWI%20Alliances.pdf>

Treaty	Nations Involved	Impact
1. The Three Emperors' League (1872)		
2. The Triple Alliance (1882)		
3. The Franco-Russian Alliance (1893)		
4. The Anglo-Japanese Alliance (1902)		
5. The *Entente* Cordiale (1904)		
6. The Anglo-Russian *Entente* (1907)		

Name: _____   Date: _____

World War I Alliances (cont.)

World War I began as a local war between Austria-Hungary and Serbia in 1914. It eventually grew into a war involving 32 countries. These countries took sides during the war, forming the Central Powers and Allied Powers. Many other countries remained neutral during the war.

Directions: Research the countries involved in World War I. Go to the two website URLs listed below. Use the information to color-code the map identifying the sides taken by each European country during the war: Central Powers—red, Allied Powers—blue, and neutral countries—yellow.

URLs: <http://www.pbs.org/greatwar/maps/maps_outbreak.html> and
<http://kids.britannica.com/elementary/art-89044/Almost-all-the-battles-of-World-War-I-were-fought>

Europe 1914

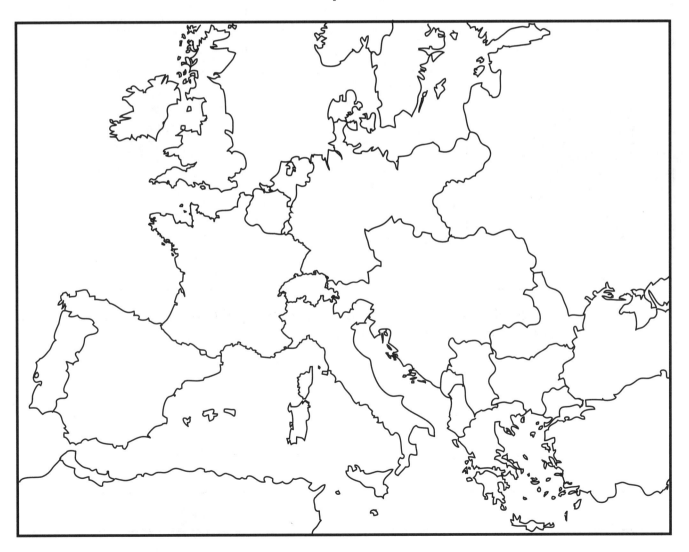

Name: _____ Date: _____

World War I Alliances (cont.)

Directions: Using the propaganda postcard found on the website, complete the *Primary Source Evaluation* chart below. The postcard is in German, but the graphics convey a very clear message.

URL: <http://publicdomainreview.org/collections/cartoon-map-of-europe-in-1914/ >

Primary Source Evaluation

What do you see?	How does this reflect the events happening in 1914?	What else would you like to know about this postcard?

What can you infer about the German reaction to the two sides of World War I? Be sure to support your answer with specific details from the postcard.

_____

_____

_____

_____

_____

Name: _____ Date: _____

Colonies of Africa 1914

Imperialism is a country gaining power by taking over other weaker countries. The taken over country becomes a **colony**.

Directions: Using the map as a guide, complete the chart, and answer the question.

URL: <http://go.grolier.com/atlas?id=mh00004>

Governing Nation	Number of Colonies
Belgium	
Britain	
France	
Germany	
Italy	
Portugal	
Spain	

The European powers met in Berlin in 1884 to make formal claims for colonies in Africa.

Positives for Governing Country	Negatives for Colony
• Obtained new territories • Controls colony's natural resources • Educate colonial people in the governing nation's language, customs, religion, dress, traditions… • Economic power over the colony • Control over new trade routes • Slave labor or cheap labor • Control over colony's military	• Loss of independence and freedoms • Loss of culture, language, religion, traditions… • Heavily taxed by governing nation • Economically dependent • Exposure to new diseases brought by the governing nation's settlers • Handmade items replaced by factory made

Using the information from the map and charts, infer why the distribution of colonies would provoke the European nations to go to war. What did they have to gain? What did they have to lose? Use textual evidence to support your answer.

_____

_____

_____

_____

_____

_____

Name: _____ Date: _____

The Von Schlieffen Plan

The Von Schlieffen Plan was a German military plan to bring war to the Allied Powers in an effort to avoid a drawn out, bloody war fought on two fronts.

Directions: Watch the Von Schlieffen Plan youtube video found at the website URL listed below. Use the information from the video to complete the "Why Did the Von Schlieffen Plan Fail?" chart.

URL: <https://www.youtube.com/watch?v=lHeMPV5VDR4> [Use lowercase L (l) in address.]

Why Did the Von Schlieffen Plan Fail?

Reason	Notes
Transportation	
Communication	
Kaiser's message	
Troops	
Russia	

Do you agree that the Von Schlieffen Plan helped cause World War I? Please use specific evidence from the video to support your answer.

_____

_____

_____

_____

_____

Name: _____ Date: _____

Trench Life

Along the Western Front, there were hundreds of miles of trenches. These trenches became the homes of Allied and Central Power soldiers alike. The trenches were muddy, smelly, rat-infested holes in the ground. Many contained human waste and numerous bodies of fallen soldiers. These were the nastiest conditions possible to live in and fight a war.

Directions: Using the website URL listed below, read the article "Life in the Trenches." Use the information from these two sources to complete the worksheet. Be sure to restate and answer in complete sentences using textual evidence to support your answer.

URL: <http://inthefootsteps.org.uk/articles/1914-18greatwar/lifeinthetrenches.htm>

1. How is World War I typified? _____

_____

_____

2. Trench warfare brought new challenges to both sides. Explain these challenges.

_____

_____

3. Explain the "Trench Cycle." _____

_____

_____

4. Explain the typical daily routine for a soldier in the trenches.

Stand To: _____

_____

_____

Morning Hate: _____

_____

_____

Name: _____ Date: _____

Trench Life (cont.)

Daily Inspection: _____

_____

_____

Daily Boredom: _____

_____

_____

Stand Down: _____

_____

_____

Sentry Duty: _____

_____

_____

5. Explain the most common causes of death while living in the trenches.

_____

_____

_____

_____

6. Why was rat infestation bad for the soldiers?

_____

_____

_____

Name: _____ Date: _____

Trench Life (cont.)

7. List several ways soldiers would try to get rid of the rats. Were these methods effective? Why or why not?

_____

_____

_____

_____

8. Summarize the lice infestations and the consequences of these infestations.

_____

_____

_____

_____

9. Describe the smell of the trenches, and explain the causes of the stench.

_____

_____

_____

_____

10. What 10 words would you use to describe life in the trenches?

Directions: On your own paper, make a word collage of the description words used above.

Name: _____ Date: _____

Differing Points of View

Directions: Read the poem "The Glory of the Trenches" found at the URL listed. Complete the questions.

URL: <http://www.pagebypagebooks.com/Coningsby_Dawson/
The_Glory_of_the_Trenches/The_Glory_Of_The_Trenches_
p1.html>

Explain the meaning of the following lines.

1. "When our poor death could dry the tears—Of little children yet unborn."

    _____

    _____

2. "When manhood's hope was at its height," _____

    _____

    _____

3. "We stopped a bullet in mid-flight." _____

    _____

    _____

4. "So long Sleep was our only cure" _____

    _____

    _____

5. "Yet loving more than home or wife—The kindness of a world set free—For countless children yet to be."

    _____

    _____

    _____

6. What was the author's opinion of the war? How do you know?

    _____

    _____

    _____

Name: _____   Date: _____

Differing Points of View (cont.)

Directions: Read the poem "Dulce et Decorum Est" by Wilfred Owen found at the URL listed and complete the questions.

URL: <http://www.warpoetry.co.uk/owen1.html#READINGS>

1. What feelings do you have while and after reading the poem?

Feeling	Lines from the poem that cause that feeling

2. The title of the poem means, "it is sweet and honorable…" The last two lines mean "it is sweet and honorable to die for one's country." Do you believe the poet truly believes his last line? Give specific examples to support your answer.

   _____

   _____

   _____

   _____

3. Which of the two poems read in this activity is your favorite? Give text-specific evidence to support your answer.

   _____

   _____

   _____

   _____

Name: _____ Date: _____

"Break of Day in the Trenches" by Isaac Rosenberg

Directions: Listen to the poem "Break of Day in the Trenches" found at the URL listed. In small groups, read the poem in sections. As each group of lines is read, write your initial thoughts: mood, descriptions, figurative language, questions, sketch image, WWI facts, etc. Discuss the group's initial thoughts. Discuss the poem.

URL: <http://www.poetryfoundation.org/poetrymagazine/poems/detail/13535>

"Break of Day in the Trenches" by Isaac Rosenberg

Lines	Initial Thoughts
Lines 1–4	
Lines 5–8	
Lines 9–12	
Lines 13–16	
Lines 17–21	
Lines 22–26	

Name: _____ Date: _____

"Break of Day in the Trenches" by Isaac Rosenberg (cont.)

Directions: Summarize the poem.

_____

_____

_____

_____

_____

_____

_____

_____

Directions: Assign the sections, already broken into sections in the chart on the previous page, so all members have at least one section and all sections are taken. Each student should illustrate their section on the bottom of this page. Be sure to write the words of the section on the bottom of each illustration. When finished, design a cover as a class or group, staple the pages together, and make a little booklet of the poem.

Name: _____ Date: _____

Unrestricted Submarine Warfare

On February 8, 1915, Germany declared "unrestricted" submarine warfare. Read Germany's proclamation.

URL: <http://wwi.lib.byu.edu/index.php/German_Admiralty_ Declaration_Regarding_Unrestricted_U-Boat_Warfare>

Directions: Use the information from the website URL listed below to create a bar graph illustrating the number of ships hit each year of the war by German U-boats.

URL: <http://www.uboat.net/wwi/ships_hit/losses_year.html>

Ships Hit by German U-boat Attacks 1914–1919

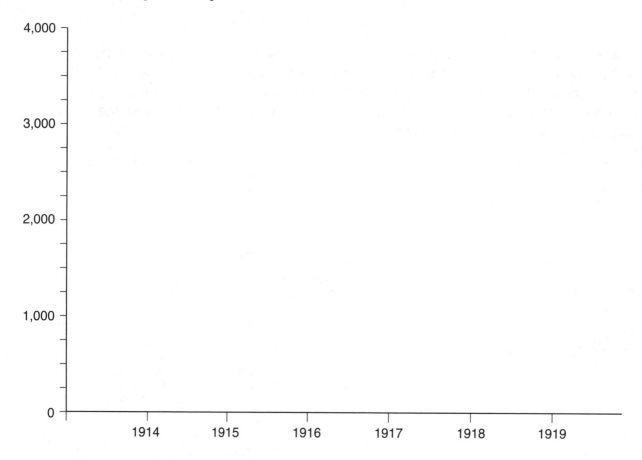

Name: _____ Date: _____

Unrestricted Submarine Warfare (cont.)

Directions: Review the maps at the website URL listed below. Become familiar with the locations, concentrations, and sizes of ships sunk by U-boats. Using the information from the websites on pg. 16, answer the following questions.

URL: <http://www.smithsonianmag.com/history/map-shows-full-extent-devastation-wrought-uboats-world-war-i-180955191/?no-ist>

Do you believe unrestricted submarine warfare was an effective method of fighting for the Germans? Why? Remember to support your opinion with evidence from the three website URLs used in this activity.

_____

_____

_____

_____

_____

_____

_____

_____

_____

_____

_____

_____

_____

_____

Name: _____ Date: _____

Weapons of World War I

Weapons during World War I ranged from tried-and-true bayonets and bolt-action rifles to cutting-edge innovations like poisonous gas, tanks, flamethrowers, and airplanes.

Directions: Research the weapons in the chart. Go online to the website URL listed below; it is a good starting point. Use the information to complete the chart.

URL: <http://www.firstworldwar.com/weaponry/>

Weapons of World War I

Weapon	Description	Advantages	Disadvantages
Machine Gun			
Zeppelin			
Mustard Gas			
Chlorine Gas			
Artillery			
Tank			
Airplanes			
U-Boats			
Torpedoes			
Bolt-action Rifle			

Name: _____   Date: _____

Weapons of World War I (cont.)

Directions: Using the website URLs listed below, browse several print advertisements available on the websites. Pay special attention to the style, color pallette, lettering, wording, and other techniques used to sell products in 1914–18. Design a print advertisement for one of the post-1900 weapons used in World War I. Be sure to include the following information: advantages of the weapon, situations where it would be used, skills needed to operate it, and new technology it uses.

URLs:<http://library.duke.edu/digitalcollections/eaa_P0097/ >
        <http://library.brown.edu/exhibits/sphere/>
        <https://www.bl.uk/world-war-one/articles/commercial-advertising-as -propaganda
        <http://library.brown.edu/exhibits/sphere/>

Name: _____ Date: _____

Weapons of World War I (cont.)

Directions: Using the information from your research, choose two post-1900 weapons that you believe made the biggest impacts during World War I. Write a paragraph using evidence from your research to support your two choices. (You may need to do additional research for information on estimated number of casualties caused by the weapons and which sides used them.)

_____

_____

_____

_____

_____

_____

_____

_____

_____

_____

_____

_____

_____

_____

_____

_____

_____

Name: _____ Date: _____

Battles of World War I

Many battles were fought during World War I. They were fought on different fronts involving several countries. The **Western Front** involved Germany's push into Belgium and France. The **Eastern Front** stretched from the Baltic Sea in the north to the Black Sea in the south. The Germans, Austro-Hungarians, and Ottomans faced the Russians and Romanians, among others. There are only three ways a battle can end: you are the winner, you are the loser, or it is a tie or **stalemate**.

Directions: Using the website URL listed below as a starting point, choose a battle from World War I. Research the battle and complete a study card below.

URL: <http://www.firstworldwar.com/battles/all.htm>.

Battle of World War I	**Battle of World War I**
Battle:_____	Battle:_____
Date started: _____	Date started: _____
Date ended: _____	Date ended: _____
Where fought (town and country): _____ _____	Where fought (town and country): _____ _____
Countries involved: _____ _____ _____	Countries involved: _____ _____ _____
Military leaders involved and their sides: _____ _____ _____ _____	Military leaders involved and their sides: _____ _____ _____ _____
Miscellaneous information: _____ _____ _____ _____ _____	Miscellaneous information: _____ _____ _____ _____ _____
Battle outcome: _____ _____ _____	Battle outcome: _____ _____ _____

Name: _____ Date: _____

Christmas Truce

The Christmas Truce of 1914 was a unique event in World War I. For 24 hours or so, there were no sniper shots, no pounding artillery, or any other signs of the bloody battles that raged up and down the Western Front.

Directions: Using the website URLs listed below, read several accounts of the 1914 Christmas Truce. Take notes on the details of the truce: which side started it, the interactions between the Allied and Central Powers, officer reactions, areas of the front that participated in the truce, soldiers' feelings, soldiers' comments, and soldiers' reactions.

URLs: Christmas truce details
- <http://news.bbc.co.uk/2/hi/special_report/1998/10/98/world_war_i/197627.stm >
- <http://www.bbc.com/news/uk-england-stoke-staffordshire-30296660>
- <http://www.dailymail.co.uk/news/article-2884479/Today-cigar-Fritz-s-best-sniper-hope-tomorrow-know-1914-Christmas-truce-extraordinary-letters-men-sides-cast-new-light-iconic-episode.html>
- <http://www.eyewitnesstohistory.com/trenches.htm>
- <http://www.theweek.co.uk/world-news/first-world-war/61816/wwi-christmas-truce-soldiers-memories-of-the-brief-peace>
- <http://www.ppu.org.uk/remembrance/xmas/xmas_tx1.html>

Directions: In small groups, write a radio drama about the Christmas truce.

URLs:
- Provides several examples of radio drama scripts: <http://emruf.webs.com/>.
- Provides examples of an actual radio drama: <http://www.radioechoes.com/the-avengers>

While writing the Christmas truce dramas, listen to the website URL listed below to find traditional European Christmas music of the time. These songs would have been the Christmas songs the soldiers would have been familiar with.

URL: <http://www.folkways.si.edu/traditional-european-christmas-music/music/playlist/smithsonian>

Name: _____ Date: _____

The United States of America's Neutrality

On August, 19, 1914, President Woodrow Wilson delivered the speech, "U.S. Declaration of Neutrality, 19 August 1914". It was a speech to Congress explaining why the United States must remain neutral.

Directions: Read President Wilson's speech at the website URL listed below and complete the questions.

URL: <http://wwi.lib.byu.edu/index.php/President_Wilson's_ Declaration_of_Neutrality>

Answer the following questions in complete sentences. Remember to restate and use textual evidence from "U.S. Declaration of Neutrality, 19 August 1914" when possible.

1. What is Wilson's definition of "true spirit of neutrality"?

_____

_____

_____

2. According to the speech, who does Wilson believe is responsible for keeping America neutral?

_____

_____

_____

3. What is Wilson's greatest fear during this time?

_____

_____

_____

_____

Name: _____   Date: _____

The United States of America's Neutrality (cont.)

4. **Directions:** Using the website URL listed below, read the article "Ethnic Minorities at War (USA)" in the *International Encyclopedia of the First World War*.

    URL: <http://encyclopedia.1914-1918-online.net/article/ethnic_minorities_at_war_usa>.

    According to the article, "By 1910, immigrants accounted for 15 percent of the United States population… When Europe went to war in 1914, fully one-third of the people living in the United States were either foreign-born or had parents born overseas." Read the article and use the information to answer the question: How did this fact affect America's neutrality?

    _____

    _____

    _____

    _____

    _____

    _____

    _____

    _____

    _____

    _____

    _____

5. In 1914, the world was in turmoil. Several countries were becoming involved in World War I. The United States declared a position of neutrality. Pretend you are a European-born United States citizen living in America with family back in Europe. On your own paper, write a letter to President Woodrow Wilson responding to his speech of neutrality. Voice your opinion on neutrality, which side we should ally with, and why they would be good allies. Remember the causes of the war, and use that information to help prove your points.

Name: _____ Date: _____

The *Lusitania*

The RMS *Lusitania* was a British ocean liner that sank off the coast of Ireland May 7, 1915. She was torpedoed by a German U-boat. Germany had warned all sea travelers, several times, that it was not safe to travel in the waters around Europe.

Directions: Look at the website URLs listed below to find out more information about the sinking of the *Lusitania*.

URLs:

- <http://chroniclingamerica.loc.gov/lccn/sn83030214/1915-02-05/ed-1/seq-1/ #words=Berlin+Decree+Declares+Waters+Around+British+Isles>
- <http://chroniclingamerica.loc.gov/lccn/sn83030214/1915-05-01/ed-1/seq-3/>
- <https://wwionline.org/articles/complex-case-rms-lusitania/>

First documentation in film of the *Lusitania* sinking.

- <https://archive.org/details/Sinking_of_the_Lusitania#>
- <http://www.firstworldwar.com/features/lusitania.htm>

Kapitanleutnant Schwieger's diary entry

- <https://www.archives.gov/exhibits/eyewitness/html.php?section=18>

Germany's response

- <http://www.firstworldwar.com/source/lusitania_germanresponse.htm>

Propaganda

- <http://americanhistory.si.edu/blog/lusitania-propaganda>
- <http://www.english.emory.edu/LostPoets/Enlist.html>

Directions: After studying the URLs, divide the class into half: Germany and United States. Divide the Germany and the United States big groups into smaller manageable groups of three to four students each. Have each small group write a newspaper article about the sinking of the *Lusitania* from the perspective of a German citizen or an American citizen.

Name: _____ Date: _____

The Zimmerman Telegram

One of the factors that led to the United States' loss of neutrality was the Zimmerman telegram.

Directions: Using the website URLs listed throughout the worksheet as research tools, complete the questions below.

URL: <https://www.archives.gov/education/lessons/zimmermann/>

Read the translation of the Zimmerman telegram found at the above website URL.

1. Write a summary of the telegram using your own words.

_____

_____

_____

_____

_____

_____

_____

_____

_____

_____

URL: <http://www.smithsonianmag.com/history/document-deep-dive-what-did-the-zimmermann-telegram-say-29792028/?no-ist>

This document allows the reader to click on the yellow highlights to discover the story of how the telegram was deciphered and reached President Wilson's hands. Explore the site and answer the questions on the following page.

Name: _____ Date: _____

The Zimmerman Telegram (cont.)

2. Why did the cryptologists find it curious that the words "Mexico" and "alliance" were found in a secret telegram from Germany to Mexico?

_____

_____

_____

_____

3. What does this quote mean? "The telegram had such an impact on American opinion that, according to David Kahn, author of *The Codebreakers*, 'No other single cryptanalysis has had such enormous consequences.'" It is his opinion that never before or since has so much turned upon the solution of a secret message.

_____

_____

_____

_____

_____

4. The famous quote, "The pen is mightier than the sword" was written by Edward Bulwer-Lytton in his play *Richelieu; Or the Conspiracy*. Do you believe that the words of the Zimmerman telegram were mightier than a sword? Be sure to give evidence to support your answer.

_____

_____

_____

_____

_____

_____

Name: _____ Date: _____

Really Neutral?

On August 19, 1914, America declared its neutrality. In his speech to Congress, President Wilson said, "Every man who really loves America will act and speak in the true spirit of neutrality, which is the spirit of impartiality and fairness and friendliness to all concerned." But was America really neutral from August 19, 1914, until its declaration of war on April 6, 1917?

Directions: Using the website URLs listed below, complete the exercises that follow.

URLs: <https://www.mtholyoke.edu/~le20j/NonNeutralityBeforeWar.html>
<https://wwi.lib.byu.edu/index.php/U.S._Policy_on_War_Loans_to_Belligerents>
<https://www.mtholyoke.edu/~le20j/EventsBeforeWar.html>

1. Using an online or print dictionary, write the definition of the word *neutral.*

_____

_____

2. Several pieces of evidence suggest that the United States was not really neutral. Summarize each piece of evidence.

Evidence	Summary
JP Morgan and Allied Nations formed bond	
War Loans	

Name: _____ Date: _____

Really Neutral? (cont.)

Evidence	Summary
Committee on Public Information	
Germany's engagement in submarine warfare	
The sinking of the *Lusitania*	
The Zimmerman telegram	

Really Neutral? (cont.)

3. Using the information from the research websites, answer this question. Do you believe the United States was neutral from August 19, 1914, to April 6, 1917? Be sure to use specific examples and evidence to support your opinion.

_____

_____

_____

_____

_____

_____

_____

_____

_____

_____

_____

_____

_____

_____

_____

_____

_____

Name: _____ Date: _____

Anti-War Movement

As war raged in Europe, not all citizens were in favor of fighting. Across Europe and America there was an anti-war movement. Groups held protests and meetings, created anti-war propaganda, and tried to influence the general population to protest the war. In the United States, this movement ignited a debate over whether it was constitutional to disagree with the president and voice your anti-war opinion.

Directions: Using the website URLs listed below, research the anti-war movement by exploring its propaganda, songs, activities, and the reasoning behind the movement.

URLs:

- <http://depts.washington.edu/antiwar/WW1_reds.shtml>
- <http://library.duke.edu/digitalcollections/hasm_a6074/>
- <https://wwionline.org/articles/opposition-war-united-states/>
- <http://blog.constitutioncenter.org/2015/05/the-world-war-i-anti-war-movement-and-the-first-amendment/>
- <http://publications.newberry.org/frontiertoheartland/items/show/66>
- <https://archive.org/details/TheDeserter>
- <https://archive.org/details/BlessedAreThePeacemakers_26>
- <http://www.resistance100.org/>

Directions: Individually or in small groups, using the information gained from the research, create an anti-war public service message for radio, newspaper, or television (even though television was not invented until 1927). Be sure to use ideas and arguments used in the actual World War I anti-war movement.

Directions: Individually or in small groups, using the information gained from the research, create an anti-war propaganda poster.

American businessman Henry Ford sponsored the Ford Peace Expedition to Europe aboard the passenger liner the Oscar II *in 1915. The ship became known as the Peace Ship. Captain G.W. Hempel (left) and Henry Ford (right)*

Name: _____ Date: _____

Wilson's Fourteen-Point Plan

On January 8, 1918, President Woodrow Wilson in a speech to Congress, presented his plan for peace. In his speech, he called his plan "The programme of the world's peace, ... the only possible programme, ..." In his eyes, it was the only way to establish world peace and keep world peace.

Directions: Using the website URLs listed below, complete the summary outline. Write a brief summary of each of the fourteen points. Use the information from the outline to create a brochure that Woodrow Wilson could have used to share his plan with members of Congress, the American public, and the leaders that would attend the eventual peace conference.

URLs:

- <http://www.american-historama.org/1913-1928-ww1-prohibition-era/fourteen-points.htm>
- <https://www.ourdocuments.gov/doc.php?doc=62&page=transcript>

President Woodrow Wilson's Fourteen Points

1. _____
   _____
   _____

2. _____
   _____
   _____

3. _____
   _____
   _____

4. _____
   _____
   _____

5. _____
   _____
   _____

Name: _____ Date: _____

Wilson's Fourteen-Point Plan (cont.)

6. _____
   _____
   _____

7. _____
   _____
   _____

8. _____
   _____
   _____

9. _____
   _____
   _____

10. _____
    _____
    _____

11. _____
    _____
    _____

12. _____
    _____
    _____

13. _____
    _____
    _____

14. _____
    _____
    _____

Name: _____ Date: _____

The Treaty of Versailles

The Great War came to an end on November 11, 1918, when in the Compiègne Forest of France, an armistice was signed by German leaders. Little did anyone know, another war between the Allied countries' diplomats was just beginning. At the Versailles Peace Conference, diplomats from all involved countries except Germany met to decide the terms of peace. The "Big 4" were Italy, Vittorio Orlando; England, David Lloyd George; United States, Woodrow Wilson; and France, Georges Clemenceau. Wilson presented his Fourteen Point Plan, but it was rejected. The "Big 4" took it upon themselves to write a treaty that would punish Germany and help the winning nations regain some of the money lost during the war. The treaty can be divided into three sections: military, territorial, and financial terms.

Directions: Using the information found at the website URL below, click on the map to complete the notes.

URL: <http://www.bbc.co.uk/schools/gcsebitesize/history/mwh/ir1/thetreatyrev1.shtml>

Alsace-Lorraine: _____

_____

The Saar: _____

_____

Rhineland: _____

_____

German Army: _____

_____

German Navy: _____

_____

German Airforce: _____

_____

Reparations: _____

_____

War Guilt: _____

_____

Name: _____   Date: _____

The Treaty of Versailles (cont.)

Polish Corridor: _____

_____

Danzig: _____

_____

German Colonies: _____

_____

The Covenant of League of Nations: _____

_____

Austria: _____

_____

Directions: Using the information from Wilson's Fourteen-Point Plan and The Treaty of Versailles, complete the chart below to compare and contrast the two plans.

Treaty of Versailles and Wilson's Fourteen Points

Treaty of Versailles Differences	Similarities	Wilson's Fourteen Points Differences

Name: _____ Date: _____

Was the Treaty of Versailles Fair?

June 28, 1919, marked the true ending of World War I. The Treaty of Versailles was signed by Germany. The Germans were expecting a very different treaty than the one they were presented. They had believed it would be based more on Wilson's Fourteen-Point Plan.

Directions: The website URLs listed below provide several examples of Germany's reaction and reasons for the reactions. Familiarize yourself with the different reactions the German people had and why they reacted this way. Using the information from the websites, complete the chart.

URLs:
- <http://www.nationalarchives.gov.uk/education/greatwar/g5/cs2/background.htm#5>
- <https://www.mtholyoke.edu/~bulin20e/classweb/consequences.html>
- <https://www.ushmm.org/wlc/en/article.php?ModuleId=10007428>
  [The last I in the address is an uppercase i (I).]

Germany's Reactions to the Treaty of Versailles

Reaction	Reason

Was the Treaty of Versailles Fair? (cont.)

Directions: Using information from your research on the Treaty of Versailles and Germany's reaction, choose either the Allied Powers' or the Central Powers' side and write a letter to the editor of a newspaper expressing your views based on the perspective of the side you have chosen.

Was the Treaty of Versailles Fair?

_____

_____

_____

_____

_____

_____

_____

_____

_____

_____

_____

_____

_____

_____

_____

_____

Name: _____ Date: _____

The Price Paid for War

World War I is called the Great War for several reasons. One reason is the large number of casualties, wounded, prisoners, and missing suffered by all countries involved. The numbers are staggering.

Directions: Using the information from the website URL listed below, complete the pie charts. Using red, color the percentage of the graph that represents the total number of casualties.

URL: <https://www.pbs.org/greatwar/resources/casdeath_pop.html>

Percentage of Casualties in Total Mobilized Forces

Russia

Great Britain

France

United States

Germany

Austria-Hungary

Draw three conclusions based on the information presented in the pie charts.

_____

_____

_____

_____

_____

Name: _____ Date: _____

Propaganda of World War I

   Propaganda is used to influence people. It is never unbiased and presents only one side's opinion. Propaganda can come in many forms: posters, commercials, billboards, songs, speeches, radio shows, etc. Citizens need to be aware that propaganda attacks them constantly. It is important to analyze propaganda before opinions are made or changed. There are several kinds of propaganda techniques listed below with a brief definition and an example of propaganda that uses that technique.

Plain Folks: identifies with common people
   <http://propaganda-poster-ww1.weebly.com/plain-folks.
   html>

Transfer or Testimonial: symbols, images, and quotes of famous people that generally have nothing to do with the issue
   <http://www.history.com/news/santa-goes-to-war>

Bandwagon: everyone is doing this
   <http://www.ww1propaganda.com/world-war-1-posters/
   american-ww1-propaganda-posters>

Glittering Generalities: using words and images that are general enough to appeal to all and promote acceptance; opposite of name-calling
   <http://www.firstworldwar.com/posters/russia.htm>

Name-Calling: largely perceived negative image; opposite of glittering generalities
   <http://propaganda-poster-ww1.weebly.com/name-calling.html>

Fear: plays on people's fears of what might happen
   <http://www.vads.ac.uk/x-large.php?uid=29494&sos=0>

Logical Fallacies: premise is accurate but the conclusion drawn is not
   <https://www.pritzkermilitary.org/explore/museum/digital-collection/view/oclc/817953762>

Directions: Use the form on the next page to analyze World War I propaganda. Examples of World War I propaganda can be found at the website URL listed below.

URL: This site has examples of propaganda from all the major fighting countries.
   <http://www.ww1propaganda.com/>

Name: _____ Date: _____

Propaganda of World War I (cont.)

1. Rough sketch of the poster

2. What is the country of origin? _____

3. What type of propaganda does this poster use?

   fear   logical fallacies   glittering generalities   name-calling

   testimonial   plain folks   bandwagon

4. What symbols, keywords, or images are used? _____

   _____

   _____

5. What is the message of this poster? _____

   _____

   _____

   _____

6. Was this poster successful in World War I? Why? _____

   _____

   _____

   _____

Name: _____ Date: _____

Remembering the War

World War I will always be a part of world history and will be remembered in many ways.

Contemporary songwriter and singer Garth Brooks helps us remember through a song, "Belleau Wood" and its video.

URL: Video: <https://www.youtube.com/watch?v= kjXa7DnaGjQ>

Lyrics: <http://www.azlyrics.com/lyrics/garthbrooks/ belleauwood.html>

Collin Raye, a popular singer and songwriter, also remembers the Christmas truce through his song and video, "It Could Happen Again."

URL: Video: <https://www.youtube.com/watch?v=fCQpNPGq_mU>

Lyrics: <http://www.azlyrics.com/lyrics/collinraye/itcouldhappenagain.html>

Singing group The Farm helps us remember through video and song with "All Together Now."

URL: Video: <https://www.youtube.com/watch?v=F7MwXniOD44&list=RDF7MwXniOD44 #t=144>

Lyrics:< http://www.songlyrics.com/the-farm/all-together-now-lyrics/>

Art also helps us remember World War I. In the article found at the website URL listed below, it explains seven ways art can help us remember.

URL: Article: <http://www.bbc.co.uk/guides/zgmq7ty>

Artwork: <http://www.smithsonianmag.com/smithsonian-institution/remembering- americas-official-artists-war-180952321/?no-ist>

<http://www.bl.uk/collection-items/villain-your-work>

<http://www.bl.uk/world-war-one/articles/why-paint-war-british-and-belgian-artists>

Directions: In small groups or individually, create a way to remember World War I. Be creative and use your unique talents. Some suggestions are listed below.

Video	Blog
Song	Powerpoint or slide presentation
Poem or a collection of poems	Graphic novel
Painting or drawing	Short story
Sculpture	Drama

Answer Keys

Answers to the activities may vary. Some possible suggestions have been included.

World War I Alliances (pg. 4)

Treaty	Nations Involved	Impact
1. The Three Emperors' League (1872)	Austria, Russia, Germany	Attempt to isolate France
2. The Triple Alliance (1882)	Germany, Austria-Hungary, Italy	Made to keep Italy from siding with Russia
3. The Franco-Russian Alliance (1893)	Russia, France	Russia and France became allies
4. The Anglo-Japanese Alliance (1902)	Japan, Britain	Britain and Japan ally Ends Britain's isolationism
5. The *Entente* Cordiale (1904)	Britain, France	Allied Britain and France Ended disputes over colonies
6. The Anglo-Russian *Entente* (1907) *Triple Entente*	Britain, France, Russia	Made because of worsening relations between Germany and Russia and Germany and Britain

Europe 1914 Map (p. 5)

Allied Powers (blue): Russia, France, Britain, Italy (1915), Rumania (Romania), Greece, Serbia, Portugal
Central Powers (red): Germany, Ottoman Empire, Austria-Hungary
Neutral (yellow): Sweden, Norway, Spain, Switzerland

Primary Source Evaluation (pg. 6)

Answers will vary.
Inference: Germany did not like the division of sides.

Colonies of Africa 1914 (pg. 7)

1. Belgium 1, Britain 14, France 6, Germany 4, Italy 3, Portugal 1, Spain 3
2. Germany had fewer colonies than Britian or France. Germany lacked the colonial military power the Allied Powers had. Allied Powers would lose all the benefits of a colony if they lost a war.

The Von Schlieffen Plan (pg. 8)
Why did the Von Schlieffen Plan Fail?

Reason	Notes
Transportation	Needed speed for success Can only go where train tracks go No plan for delays and replacing tracks—French destroyed tracks
Communication	Same technical level as other countries Radios and telegraphs were scarce at front Used flags and pigeons at front—reports were not accurate and in real time
Kaiser's message	False message that France was not mobilizing Wanted all troops to Russia
Troops	Casualties could not be replaced Reserves were not properly trained
Russia	Dismissed as a strong enemy Mobilized before France

Cause of World War I: Answers may vary

Trench Life (pg. 9–11)
1. Lack of movement and stalemate
2. Fighting and simply trying to live
3. A spell at the front; a stint in the support lines; a period in reserve; rest
4. Stand To: One hour before dawn, fixed bayonets and prepared for enemy raid
   Morning Hate: Release tension, random firing of weapons and artillery at enemy
   Daily Inspection: Guns cleaned in shifts, weapons and clothes inspected, trench-foot inspections
   Daily Boredom: Time fillers during the inactive times: reading, writing letters, sleeping, cards
   Stand Down: At dusk, same as Stand To
   Sentry Duty: Patrolling the perimeters, 20-hour shifts, if fall asleep—death by firing squad
5. Artillery bursts, rifle shots, buried alive, sniper, looking over the top of the trench, disease
6. Carried diseases, fed on the dead, raided food supplies, kept soldiers up at night
7. Gun fire, bayonets, clubbing, rat terriers, rat hunts—a pair of rats can produce over 900 babies a year
8. 97% of soldiers got lice, body lice or head lice, causes itching, could cause trench fever: painful and high fever, up to 12 weeks to recover, spread by blood obtained in lice bites
9. Putrid, stench caused by the smell of rotting flesh: unburied men left in No Man's Land for days; overflowing latrines; unclean men stinking; disinfectant; battle smells
10. Answers may vary.

Differing Points of View (pg. 12–13)
"Glory of the Trenches" by Coningsby Dawson
1. The soldier's death could save future generations heartache and tears because justice won.
2. When soldiers were the most hopeful for victory
3. The soldiers were shot.
4. The only way out of the misery was death.
5. The soldiers love their homes and lives, but they feel the cause is more important for future generations.
6. The author is very proud to be a soldier and fighting for the cause. The soldier does not like the war and its consequences.
"Dulce et Decorum Est" by Wilfred Owen
1. Answers may vary.
2. Answers may vary.
3. Answers may vary.

"Break of Day in the Trenches" by Isaac Rosenberg (pg. 14–15)
Initial Thoughts: Answers may vary.
Summary: The poem is about a man in the trenches in the morning. A rat touches him and the soldier thinks about what the rat may see if he were in different trenches. Would it be the same? Better? Worse? The soldier also feels that the rat is laughing at him.

Unrestricted Submarine Warfare (pg. 16–17)
Bar graphs should reflect these numbers:
    1914: 15   1915: 756   1916: 1,516   1917: 3,722   1918: 1,646   1919: 2
Answers to opinion paragraph will vary.

Weapons of World War I (pg. 18–20)

Weapon	Description	Advantages	Disadvantages
Machine Gun	-On stand -Rapid fire -Requires a team to run	-400 rounds per minute -Fire power of 100 guns -Shells explode on impact	-Easily jams -4-6 men to run -Must be on a flat surface
Zeppelin	-Blimp -12 tons -400,000 cu.ft. of hydrogen	-Bombing raids -Basically silent -4,400 lbs. of bombs	-Easy to shoot down -Weather
Mustard Gas	-Poisonous gas -Most deadly	-Odorless and powerful -Small amount needed -Added to shells -Active several weeks	-Wind direction -12 hours to take effect -Skin blisters, sore eyes, vomiting
Chlorine Gas	-Poisonous gas -Distinctive smell (pineapple/pepper)	-Death is painful; suffocation -Death is quick	-Weather conditions -Urine-soaked cotton pads neutralize
Artillery	-Large-caliber guns	-Long range -Huge payload	-Inaccurate -Slow
Tank	-Rolling artillery -Crew of 3 -10 mph -Revolving turret	-Armored -Mobile -Protection for attacking soldiers	-Speed -Difficulties in mud and unlevel terrain (tracks)
Airplanes	-Open cockpit plane	-Deliver bombs, machine guns, cannons -Reconnaissance work	-Dogfights -New technology used in warfare
U-Boats	-German submarines	-Sneak attacks	-Mechanical problems
Torpedoes	-Used by German submarines	-One torpedo could sink a ship	-If misses, it is lost
Bolt-action Rifle	-Individual weapon -Bolt action operates	-Mobile	-Easily jams -Difficult for left-handers to use

Impacts: Answers may vary.

The United States of America's Neutrality (pg. 23–24)
1. The spirit of impartiality and fairness and friendliness to all concerned
2. Individuals, society, those gathered in public meetings, newspapers, magazines, ministers...
3. Division among Americans concerning which side to support
4. Answers may vary.
   - Government unsure of non-citizen immigrants loyalty
   - Language barriers—prohibits effective communication
   - Immigrants clung to old beliefs, languages, customs, traditions, and religion
   - Neighbor not trusting neighbor
   - Protests
   - Switching allegiances
   - Ethnic civil war
5. Answers may vary.

The Zimmerman Telegram (pg. 26–27)
1. Summary: It was a secret telegram from Germany to Mexico asking Mexico to attack the United States. In exchange, for attacking the United States on its own soil, Germany would give Mexico Texas, Arizona, California, and New Mexico. Was intercepted by the British. Helped sway America into joining the war on the Allied side.

2. Germany and Mexico were not allies. Mexico was not involved in the war.
3. The quotation means that the telegram insulted the Americans to think Mexico would invade to keep them out of the war. It is given as the "straw that broke the camel's back" in getting America involved. This telegram affected basically every person in the world because it really made World War I a world war.
4. Answers may vary.

Really Neutral? (pg. 28–30)
1. Answers will vary, but should be similar to: not helping or supporting either side in a conflict, disagreement, etc.; impartial
2.

Evidence	Summary
JP Morgan and Allied Nations formed bond	-Loaned $2.3 billion to Allied Powers: Russia 12 million and France 50 million -Countries used money for war supplies -Played major role in the Great War
War Loans	-At beginning of war, U.S. did not believe in loaning to warring countries. -In Aug. 1914, prominent men started a discussion with President Wilson about changing the policies on war loans -War loans gave the impression of intervening instead of neutral -Decided if "we" don't know about it, it is ok. -America tended to favor countries that owed the most money
Committee on Public Information	-Executive Order 2594 -Basically a propaganda department -Used all aspects of media -"Four-minute men" -Changes America's views of interventionism and promoted anti-German feelings
Germany's engagement in submarine warfare	-At first honored neutral flags -Unconditional warfare: no one safe -Violated America's neutral rights
The sinking of the *Lusitania*	-Killed innocent and neutral Americans: women and children -Promoted anti-German feelings -Influenced America into joining the war
The Zimmerman telegram	-Americans mad…. How dare they even think about it! -Influenced America to join the war

3. Essay: Answers may vary.

Wilson's Fourteen-Point Plan (pg. 32–33)
1. No private international understanding—diplomacy frank and in public view
2. International waters open to navigate during war and peace
3. Free trade with countries at peace
4. Arms reduction—worldwide
5. Impartial adjustment of colonial claims
6. Russia will be free to choose its own government—German troops will evacuate
7. German troops will leave Belgium, and Belgium will be an independent country.
8. France will get back all disputed lands of Alsace-Lorraine.
9. Italy's frontiers should be adjusted to reflect clear lines of nationality.
10. Austria-Hungary—independent country
11. Occupied territories of Romania, Serbia, and Montenegro—evacuated and independent countries
12. Turkish people will have their own country.
13. Establishment of independent Poland
14. League of Nations

The Treaty of Versailles (pg. 34–35)
Alsace-Lorraine: Alsace-Lorraine returned to France
The Saar: given to France for 15 years
Rhineland: demilitarized—German army was not allowed there
Army: reduced to 100,000 men
Navy: reduced to only six battle ships and no submarines
Airforce: not allowed to have one
Reparations: pay back for damages caused by war
War Guilt: take total blame for all loss and damage caused by war
Polish Corridor: Eastern Germany given to Poland
Danzig: free city controlled by League of Nations
German Colonies: taken away and given to Britain and France
The Covenant of League of Nations: formed league and Germany not allowed to join
Austria: forbidden to unite

Treaty of Versailles and Wilson's Fourteen Points (pg. 35)

Treaty of Versailles	Similarities	Wilson's Fourteen Points
-War Guilt Clause -Germany's military limits -Large reparations -Germany's colonies taken -Germany's land divided and turned into independent countries -Danzig -Austria	-Alsace-Lorraine returned to France -Formation of the League of Nations	-Open diplomacy -Freedom of navigation -Multilateral disarmament -Russia -Italy -Romania, Montenegro, and Serbia -Turkey -Poland

Was the Treaty of Versailles Fair? (pg. 36–37)

Reaction	Reason
Upset, Frustrated, Helpless, Angry, Hopeless, Mad	-Lost all of their colonies -Reduction of military -Loss of land -Had to pay Allies for loss and damages
Patriotic	-Still felt Germany was a great country and never lost their sense of pride
Revengeful	-Needed to prove to the world that Germany would once again be great

Letter to the Editor: Answers may vary.

The Price Paid for War (pg. 38)

Russia: 76.3%   Great Britain: 35.8%   France: 73.3%
United States: 7.1%   Germany: 64.9%   Austria-Hungary: 90%

Generalizations: Answers may vary. Reasons may be used in class discussion at the end of the activity.
 -United States had the lowest percent of casualties because they did not join the fighting until 1917.
 -Austria-Hungary had the highest percentage of casualties.
 -Both Central Powers and Allies had close to the same percentages of casualties.

Remembering the War (pg. 41)
Projects will vary. Encourage students to use their imaginations and talents.